DAYS IN DEVONPORT
PART II

Gerald W. Barker

Boer War Memorial, Devonport Park

The author with two small visitors from Torpoint are here next to this familiar memorial in the park. It was here in 1933 that a small tribute was paid by Mr. Thomas Roberts, chairman of the Street Decorations Display Committee for the Carnival, who served in the Boer War. He laid a wreath on behalf of the Entertainments Committee on the memorial as a mark of respect to his Devonport comrades who fell during the South African War.

This version of the book is virtually as originally published, presenting the work of Gerald W Barker. There are now additional pages at the back providing information about the publisher, Arthur L Clamp.

The republishing project is being managed by Arthur's grandson, Steven Gibson. We aim to find all the research that he was involved in publishing, preserving it for the next generation as part of 'The Clamp Collection'.

INTRODUCTION

CAN YOU tell from the following paragraph which year it is?

"Devonport people are a long-suffering body. We have stood quietly by and seen thousands and thousands of pounds spent on the other end of the city. Some of it has been wasteful expenditure. I could name one or two places which are no earthly good for the money spent on them. I ask you to stop spending so much at the other end, and spend a little more this end. The Devonport end of the city is as rich in its historical associations as the other part, and, because of that I think any reasonable claim which we make should be given a most sympathetic hearing."

Was the date 1980? 1960? Before? It was, in fact, in 1933, when Sir William Mounstephen made the criticism when presenting a silver cup given by Mr. Leslie Hore-Belisha, M.P. for Devonport, for competition among members of Devonport Park Bowling Club.

The late Councillor, P. Washbourn, who was a member of the city council since 1939 and Lord Mayor 1959-60 and owned a number of shops in Tavistock Street, Cumberland and Market Street, was critical of the way that any chance of rebuilding Devonport after the war was thwarted. He remarked that Devonport had been the most efficient and least costly of the Three Towns. It had had its own gas undertaking which was one of the cheapest in the country.

Many Devonport citizens to whom I have spoken believed Devonport had had a raw deal! Mrs. L. M. Hooper, for example, who fought so hard to preserve St. Mary's Church from destruction in the 1950s. She had no wish to be moved out to one of the outlying estates and she lives today in George Street, Devonport.

One of the reasons for compiling *Days in Devonport* is to recall the days when Devonport was a thriving community with its own theatre and numerous cinemas. A time when hundreds upon hundreds of people thronged through Fore Street, and crowds gathered in Devonport Park to listen to the bands and enjoy the entertainment offered by the many concert parties.

When war came the citizens of Devonport helped each other to overcome the results of the devastation of their houses and places of work. During the height of the air raids a young man could be seen running along the tops of the houses in Milne Place with buckets of water to help put out the fire started by incendiary bombs. The calm voice of one of the older generation, Mr. Wilkes an Air Raid Warden, could be heard in the public air-raid shelter of Devonport Park, above the noise of the guns and falling bombs. He worked in the Dockyard during the day and gave much voluntary time to being a councillor.

I have had the pleasure of meeting many interesting people, who lived in Devonport, during the gathering of material for Part II. Mrs. Mills, for example, can remember being present at the unveiling of the Captain Robert F. Scott memorial at Mount Wise, seeing the Queen of Roumania when she visited Fore Street, been a Geraldine Lamb's dancer, and one of the ladies-in-waiting for the Carnival Queen in 1933.

I would like to thank those that have helped by loaning their photographs or by recalling events of their days in Devonport. Among these are: Mr. K. Oram, Mr. T. McCarthy, Mrs. K. Mills, Mr. B. Mills, Mr. S. Dilling, Mr. T. Lillicrap, Mr. G. Scantlebury, Mrs. M. Wills, Mrs. D. Paramore, Mrs. Bright, Mr. R. Smith, Mrs. L. M. Hooper, Mrs. L. M. Duddleston, Mrs. M. Laxton, Mr. R. Watkins, Geraldine Lamb (Sylvia and Valerie), Mr. A. C. Barker and Mr. P. F. Ghillyer.

Days in Devonport, Part I, was launched with the indispensable help of Arthur L. Clamp's expertise, Part II is ready to set sail and already material is at hand for a Part III. Thank you, therefore, to all who have contributed in the preparation of Part I and II and please continue to search your lofts and cupboards for material for Part III.

Gerald W. Barker,
44 Burnham Park Road,
Peverell, Plymouth.
Telephone 784725

Appendix to Part I

Page 8: This should read King George VI coronation.

Page 23: The mayor was Alderman Littleton.

Page 23: Richard's shop. Mr. Ghillyer remembers this shop in Queen Street next door to old "Daddy's Pesters" toffee shop where he made all his own sweets.

Page 24: The "P" was Prynns the gent's outfitters. It was a mecca for Devonport people as the shop took providence cheques from the poorer families.

Poor Man's Corner: This is in Richmond Walk in the vicinity of the new marina.

Page 6: Queen Street ran parallel to King Street.

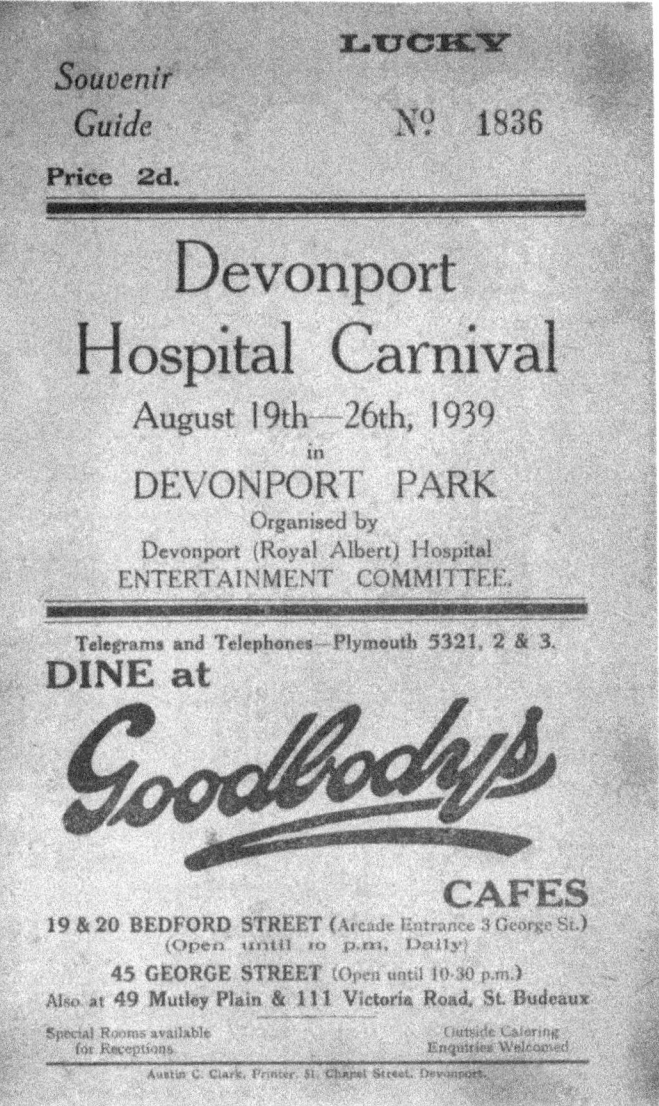

Devonport Carnival Feature

"QUEEN'S" MOTOR TOUR OF CITY

Children in Fancy Dress Contest

THOSE who attended the Devonport (Royal Albert Hospital) Carnival in Devonport Park last night had an opportunity of witnessing an advance showing of autumn wear, for one of yesterday's features was a mannequin parade by Messrs. J. C. Tozer, of Devonport.

Other items were a gymnastic display by children from the Royal Dockyard Orphanage, under the direction of Mr. A. Day, a children's fancy dress parade, and a dancing display by the pupils of Miss Alma Down.

There were also alfresco concerts by the "Stars on Parade" party, a bowling match for the Royal Albert Hospital Challenge Cup, and an alfresco dance, with music by the Devon (Fortress) Royal Engineers.

The "Queen" and her "Court" were present during the first part of the evening entertainments, being obliged to leave before the conclusion in order to be present at the presentation of the Hore Belisha Cup to Devonport Park Bowling Club, to replace the one given by Sir Samuel Gluckstein, which has been won outright.

During the afternoon the "Queen" and her suite made a successful motor tour of the city.

Goodbye to the Carnivals

The 1939 carnival was the last before war was declared. Soon public air raid shelters and static water tanks would be built in Devonport park. There would be no more dancing until the victory dances of 1945. These took place in the nissen huts built in the vicinity of the bandstand by the American soldiers who occupied the park.

When & Where to see the Carnival Queen
and her Court.

Monday, 21st August

The Hospital Queen 1939, will leave the Prince of Wales's Hospital, Devonport, at 2-30 p.m. for Devonport Park via Marlborough Street and Fore Street.

After Opening Ceremony, will return the same route and visit the Wards of the Prince of Wales's Hospital, Devonport.

7-30 p.m. By kind invitation of the Manager, The Hippodrome, Devonport, the Queen and her Court will visit this Cinema,

Tuesday, 22nd August

2-30 p.m. Leave the Hospital via Marlborough St., Catherine St., James Street, Pembroke St., George St., Devonport Hill, High St., Stonehouse, King St., Cecil St., Wyndham St., Eldad Hill, Wilton St., Pennycomequick, Alma Road, Milehouse, St. Hilary Terrace, Tavistock Road, Fore St., Chapel St., Cumberland St., Tavistock St., King St., Morice Square.

7-30 p.m. The Management of the Regent Cinema, Plymouth, has kindly invited the Queen and Court to visit them.

Wednesday, 23rd August

2-30 p.m. Visit to the Prince of Wales's Hospital, Greenbank Road, and the Prince of Wales's Hospital, Lockyer St., after which a tour of the Hoe Front and Tinside.

6-30 p.m. Mount Wise Swimming Baths.

7-30 p.m. Mr. Wally Rice, Owner and Licensee of the Alhambra Theatre, Devonport, has kindly invited the Queen and Court to that Theatre.

Thursday, 24th August

2-30 p.m. Leave the Hospital via Marlborough Street, Fore Street, Tavistock Road, Stoke, Milehouse, St. Levan Road, Morice Town, Albert Road and thence to Devonport Park.

6- 0 p.m. The Management of the Forum Theatre will be pleased to entertain the Queen and her Court.

7-30 p.m. The Management of the Electric Theatre will be pleased to entertain the Queen and her Court during the evening performance.

Friday, 25th August

2-30 p.m. Leave the Hospital for a tour of Swilly, Weston Mill Estate and Higher and Lower St. Budeaux.

8-45 p.m. By the kind invitation of Mrs. Hoyle, will attend the 2nd House at the Palace Theatre, Plymouth.

Saturday, 26th August

2-30 p.m. To tour City and visit homes of the Queen and Court.

Will be in the Park Enclosure each evening from 6 p.m. to time of leaving for above visits.

A Well Known Comedian

Mike Cook was well liked by the Devonport crowds who laughed at his antics in numerous sketches on the bandstand in Devonport Park. Many were sitting in the paid seats, while others stood on the outside of the railings. The man with the box, however, made sure that the "frees" had the opportunity of contributing towards the funds of Devonport Hospital.

Where is She?

A great gathering of people would sway and push, stand on tip toe and crane their necks in Devonport Park to catch a glimpse of the pretty Carnival "Queen" and her ladies-in-waiting. Some of those present are Joyce Creber (sister of Alderman Creber), Marie Jago, Avis Styles, Barbara Tulivey, Joan Ball and Hazel Edwards.

The Queen

Having descended from the motor-cars, in which they had driven from the hospital, the "Royal" Suite would make a pretty group as they made their way to the raised dais, where a throne, upholstered in red velvet, would await "Her Majesty elect". After being crowned Queen, the carnival would be declared open.

1933 Crowning

The Queen Miss Laura Oldham, "modest, shy, and sweet seventeen, had never previously entered for a beauty competition and was surprised and pleased that she had been chosen Carnival Queen (points 12,998). Her maids received the following points: Miss E. Eileen Barnett 12,675 points, Miss Dorothy Mandrey 12,255 points, Miss Phyllis Bernie 11,401 points, Miss Kathleen Ketteridge 11,008 points.

The Concert Party

Mike Cook, the comedian who had the crowd soon laughing with his sketches, is second from left in the back row. Jack Sobey, who was in charge, played the banjo and shook the collecting box in between acts. Others remembered are Ethel Williamson, pianist, Sam and Edie Mayers, man and wife who played the piano and sang, Roy Hicks, the female impersonator and Alf Sobey who played the guitar. Talent competitions used to be a great favourite with the crowds that thronged the bandstand.

Lieut.-Comdr. R. C. WARD, c.c.,
Chairman.   R.N. (Retd.)

Mr. A. E. TAYLOR, c.c.,
Vice-Chairman.

The Rt. Hon. The LORD St. LEVAN, c.p., c.v.o.,
President.

Mr. L. SOUTHERN,
Hon. Treasurer.

Cd.-Tel. T. C. ADAMS, R.N. (Retd.)
Hon. Organising Secretary.

Chinese Costume, 1929

1929 Devonport Carnival: Mrs. Wills née Mavis Crozier won a big clock and first prize for the Chinese Costume. This had been brought back by her father from his Royal Naval Commission of two and a half years in China. Miss Crozier's sister, Nina, is seated. The prize was presented in Ker Street Guildhall before the carnival opening in Devonport Park.

Never Too Young!

The well known Geraldine Lamb dancers were hard workers during Carnival Weeks. They were always a favourite with the crowd, young and old alike. The Devonport (Royal Albert Hospital) which depended on voluntary contributions, owed a lot to such youngsters in the raising of money. Some names remembered are Valerie Tout, Sylvia Tout, Margaret Bullard and Delphie Packwood.

Pottery Quay Carnival, 1931

The King was Harry Swabey and his Queen was Olive Harris. The Mayor, Clifford Tozer, is accompanied by his wife. The small girl's surname, who is holding a cushion for the crown, is Marks. Dorothy Wyatt is on the left of the Queen and the Rev. Atherton, of St. James the Great, is in the picture. Blooms, the Naval Tailors of William Street, has his daughter on the left. Mrs. Dorothy Paramore, who lived in Gloucester Street, remembers men of about twenty years of age from Moon and John Street, with paper oranges on trees and streamers, going around the houses on Boxing Day singing and collecting for Devonport Hospital.

Take Your Litter Home!

It was one of the jobs of the boys, who proudly wore a "helpers" badge, to clear up the litter after a performance on stage in the enclosure. A more arduous task was to collect all the chairs at the beginning of carnival week from the new swimming baths at Mount Wise and carry them up to a lorry waiting by the Scott Memorial. Numerous tents had to be erected in the park as well. Ted Tout, son of Geraldine Lamb, Russell Gaylard, Roy Guard, Marie Jago, Geraldine Lamb, with her hat on and her head turned away, Mrs. Davy, known as Trixie, and Ken Headon, the present town crier of Plymouth, form part of this group.

Tivoli Continuous Pictures

"The big picture is about to start!" Mr. A. Rickard remembers Harry Harcourt, trilby on head and long coat, shouting to passers-by. Mr. P. Ghillyer, who as a boy rewound the old silent nitrate films, remembers the Dockyardies leaving Fore Street gates and going straight to the Tivoli with their lunch baskets to see the 1926 Conan Doyle's story, *The Lost World*.

Mutton Cove in the early 1930s

Mr. "Darby" Allen is in the trilby hat. Note the *First and Last* public house in the village harbour which was formerly the *Waterman's Arms*. It was turned into rented accommodation and at the time of this photograph was occupied by John H. Bromley and his family. The roof with the numerous small windows is the no. 1 slip inside the Dockyard. A fatal accident occurred on the 24th February, 1885, when Richard Brealey was engaged with R. W. Winter, of Garden Street, Morice Town, upon its large roof. A high wind caught a sheet of metal he was carrying and blew him off. He died in the Royal Hospital, Devonport. Both men were in the employ of Mr. David Sale.

George (Tich) Fleming

One of the many workers in Devonport Dockyard. Shown here in 1907 the waistcoat watch and chain were traditional wear of the period.

His wife, Clara, was the owner of a family boat hire business started by her father at Bromley Cottages, Mount Wise, in 1860. Nearby was Blagdon's boat hire. Mr. Ghillyer remembers hiring a boat for 6d. a half an hour. Old man Bladgon would stand on his little wooden structure of a pier and blow his bugle to remind people that their time was up.

Clara Victoria Fleming

Born 1859, died 1940. Most Devonport people that frequented Richmond Walk would remember the little sweet shop situated between Blagdon's boat hire and Fleming's boat hire.

Her Vantas drinks and large selection of sweets were popular with the children, especially the boys who had just completed a game of five stones and a dip in the old swimming baths nicknamed "Pikeys", which was for males only.

Three Towns Dairy, 1930s

The milkman in charge is Mr. William Woods. He is in charge of a float owned by Three Towns Dairy. He was a close friend of Mr. Sydney Dilling's uncle, Mr. James Mumford who used to live on Mutley Plain. The giant milk churn had measures of milk taken from it and decanted into jugs. Does anyone recognise the name? Does anyone recognise the name on the shop?

Clogs Will Be Worn!

The girls in clogs and aprons were bottle washers. They worked in such breweries in Devonport, Plymouth and Stonehouse in the late 1920s. Those living in Devonport, and wishing to work in Stonehouse Brewery, had to pay their ½d. at the toll gate on the bridge. Recognised are Emily Ballyntine, Polly Perkins and Miss Williams.
Who are the others?

Where's Your Half penny?

Mr. Tim McCarthy remembers as a boy his efforts to play football at the Brickfields without paying his half-penny at the toll gate on the bridge. Before 1924, when it discontinued, the boys tried to hide from the ticket collector, Maudie Birchill, by running along behind the trams.

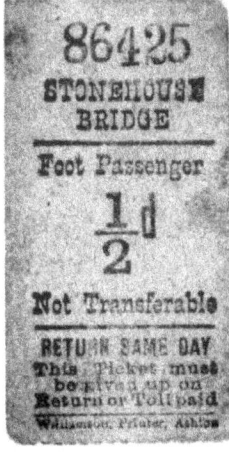

Time Running Out

Seven years left before Devonport is amalgamated in 1914, with Stonehouse and Plymouth.

Fire! Fire!

A fire at the *Crown and Column* brought many onlookers to the scene at the top of Ker Street. Before Devonport had its Guildhall (on the right), the town hall was a small building in the nearby Duke Street. It was in immediate contact with the old workhouse whose 300 inmates were employed in picking oakum for the Dockyard.

Blockhouse Air Raid Wardens

The boy holding the tin hat with "M" on its front was a messenger boy during the 1939-45 war. The air raid wardens at the Blockhouse wardens' post were: Back row, left to right, Messrs. Edgecumbe, Mill, Hearn, Renshaw, Baker and Opie. Seated: Not known: Miss Paige, Mr. Field and Mr. Bustin. It is believed that Messrs. Edgecumbe, Mill, Hearn and Renshaw worked in the Dockyard and Mr. Baker was a bus inspector, Mr. Field, the head warden, had a shop in Stoke.

Albert Road in the 1930s

It was down this road on their way to France in 1939 that company after company of soldiers marched. Assistants from shops, such as Baskervilles, would run across the road to give each leading soldier a bag of cakes. Later it was the turn of the Polish sailors whose fine voices could be heard in Milne Place and beyond as they sang on their way to work in the Dockyard. Their base was in the old female orphanage at the top of Albert Road.

Devonport Station

This station was opened on 4th May, 1859. It was built to serve the independent town of Devonport. It was known as *Devonport Albert Road* in 1948 after nationalisation to "separate" it from the Southern Station. Note the back of St. Michael's Church on the right, and the row of hoardings in the front which advertised everything from *Lux* to the *Radio Times*.

Plymouth's Four-in-One-School

To be opened today, 14th February, 1939. Each of the four schools to preserve its separate identity, with its own headmaster. Here are the men in charge. From left: Mr. G. W. Turpitt, B.Sc. (Junior Technical), Mr. T. Willcocks, F.L.S. (Tamar Central), Mr. F. S. Blight (Stoke Senior) and Mr. H. G. Taylor (Valletort Senior). The four schools are housed together in one great group of buildings—the old military hospital at Stoke.

Mayflower Pageant, 1920

Many Devonport people, such as Mrs. M. Laxton, took part in this pageant. It was staged at the Drill Hall, Millbay Park. The hall was blitzed in World War Two. More than 300 people took part and supplied their own costumes. The pageant master, Mr. Charles Richards, has a shock of white hair, and is in a smock.

Keppel Place School

This final group photograph of all the staff and pupils is w
during the last few weeks of the school on the roof of wh
Place and Regent Street schools were amalgamated to f
School. This Devonport school goes back to 1821, founded a
Higher School. Another change in title occurred in 1907 t
Keppel Place Central School. The staff in this photograp
James, Prior, Lucas, Williams, Brown, Willcocks, Syner,
The pupils are too numerous to name but you may recognis
the whole assembly brought to an end one chapter in the ed

, Devonport, 1926

orthy of occupying two pages in this book. It was taken
at is now Stoke Damerel High School for Girls. Keppel
form Sutton Secondary School, renamed Sutton High
s Stoke Public School, then in 1876 renamed Stoke Public
o Devonport Higher Elementary School then in 1922 to
h are: A. L. Stranchan, headmaster, Messrs. Swanson,
, Algate, Kemble, Gibsoh, Frost, Blackmore and Dean.
se a few here. The five shields are proudly on display and
ucational life of the people of Devonport.

Due to the current publishing methods being used,
we couldn't link these pages properly.
Apologies.

I REMEMBER (Pre-1914 Devonport)

Majorie Laxton

I remember at the age of two living in a house in George Street, Devonport, at the Mount Wise end. Mother rented two rooms at the top; the bedroom at the back holds vivid memories for me. I remember summer time, looking out from the four large windows watching the people and cricketers playing and children in the gardens. Autumn and winter evenings fascinated me for while my father was at sea I slept in the large double bed which had a black frame with brass knobs kept shiny by my mother. Bedtime was about 5.45 p.m. and before sleep overtook me I recall pulling faces at the brass knobs which gave contorted reflections and amused me.

As evening came on, the trams rattled down over the hill towards the halfpenny gate on Stonehouse bridge and I remember lying in bed watching the coloured sparks which seemed to come from the top of the trees, red, green and blue caused by the trolley arm passing the points on the overhead wires. I remember a brother, who only lived six months, after which we moved next door where my great aunt was cared for by my mother. I remember the church opposite, St. Stephens, and could hear the organ playing and the congregation singing.

I loved to trundle my wooden hoop across Mount Wise parade as far as the old gun which fired at one o'clock each day, and came to know many of the navy men and sentries from the offices. On special occasions, when visitors stayed at Admiralty House and a ball was held, I remember the thrill I had watching the ladies and gentlemen alighting from their horse-drawn carriages, the gents in their medal-bedecked uniforms and swords (sometimes) and the ladies resplendent in gorgeous gowns and sparkling tiaras on their heads.

I remember the Prince of Wales with his brother, George as I was on my way home from school and was just turning into the Lines when the sentry stopped me and a car came in and there they were, in an open car, on their way to the Raglan officers' quarters. I couldn't get home fast enough to tell everybody. Another time the Queen of Rumania visited the Commander-in-Chief and I stood besides the sentry box. She was a really regal lady in an expensive blue gown. I noticed her beautiful dark hair, a contrast to mine which was very fair and she gave me a lovely smile which made my day.

I also remember the shops in Clowance Street, a little general one ran by Victorian-type ladies called Ellis. Here could be bought anything from a gob-stopper to a piece of elastic or a bundle of wood and the mixture gave the same sort of smell as an old village shop. Next door was Davey the Baker and here folks could take their dinner to be cooked. I remember going to the bakehouse at the back and marvelling at the huge ovens and enjoying the lovely smell of bread and saffron cake.

At the age of seven, I joined St. Stephen's School where the headmistress was as much feared as disliked and the boys used to chant, *Our head teacher goes to church four times every Sunday, prays to God to give her strength to cane us kids on Monday.* These same rascals used to chase a cripple known as "Loppy Thomas" owing to the fact that his wooden leg was a bit short. They would get fairly close behind him and shout rude remarks until he could stand it no longer. He would wheel around suddenly, swearing like a trooper, and threaten them with his crutch.

I remember Pembroke Street, many pubs, many poor families, also good business people like Viggers Dairy, Alfords the Grocers and Mrs. Broom's cook shop where beef and pork were cut from the cooked joints on the counter and hogs puddings and sausages were always fresh. Joining James Street was the Pembroke Street Post Office, a hive of industry where the servicemen and fishermen would come from ashore at Mutton Cove and then call into the office to send a postcard home before spending their money liberally in the many pubs on their way to Aggie Weston's Home. At Christmas time I remember the wonderful display of fancy cakes, some made like baskets of fruit, log cakes of all sizes. This was at Palletts the Baker in George Street and people used to come from far and near to see and order.

Devonport was a thriving town with everything there anyone could wish for — a lovely market boasting its square clock and separate spaces for meat and fish, upstairs was the butter and cheese, the display of all country produce on the ground floor was wonderful even to the Wainwright's toffee stall where various toffees were set out on large trays and the slabs were cracked with a hammer as required.

I remember the old cabby, Mr. Maunder, who used to stand with his horse and cab outside Cumberland Gardens opposite the old Chapel. There was the shoemaker family who ran the Lethbridge's leather shop. I was intrigued as some of the family were deaf and dumb and I often stayed peering into the windows watching them communicating in their sign language.

Fore Street had every kind of shop from the general Post Office on the corner of Chapel Street, to the 6½d. bazaar where yellow mixing bowls and glass of all descriptions was sold; then Coombes the Optician, the Herald office, Tozers the Drapers whose premises stretched up through Marlborough Street into Granby Street. The *Royal Hotel* was down towards the Dockyard end and I remember Lord and Lady Jackson arriving here in their carriage just before hundreds of dockyardies swarmed out from the yard at 5 p.m., many on bikes, the others rushing to catch the trams to Stoke, Millbay and Plymouth.

On Christmas eve, mother would take me to see the shops with fairy lights where toys would hang outside the windows. I remember the wooden engines and rag dolls and, one year, Boulds had a Michelin tyre figure in their window which was inflated and moved up and down. His name was *Billy-By-Bendum* and he was a great attraction.

I can recall Blagdon's boatyard at Richmond Walk, where men could hire a boat for an hour or two to go fishing, then bring the fish ashore to sell and often the fish were still flapping about in the basket. Every week a man used to come around with his pony and cart selling salt which would be cut as required. The cart was covered with a tarpaulin and looked like a tent. Mother would buy a large block for 1d. I remember the organ grinder with his barrel organ and the little monkey on top; also the rag man who gave children a balloon or packet of sherbet in exchange for old clothes. These things I clearly remember, the annual service review held in the Brickfields, a colourful spectacle with the bright uniforms, decorated horses, bands playing, stalls selling paper hats, union jacks, toy bugles, ice cream carts where ½d. would buy a generous cornet. A day with a carnival atmosphere everybody enjoyed.

When I was eight years of age, my mother was taken ill and the 1914 war broke out on 4th August. I well remember the soldiers running through the streets calling out, *War declared, War declared*, which proved a very sharp experience for me, but from then onwards my memories would fill a book.

My writing is poor owing to arthritis in fingers.

1978. Mrs. M. Laxton, 72 years of age
33 Derry Avenue,
North Road East,
Plymouth.

Railway Boundary Mark

This is laid into the pavement close to the Exmouth Hall and shows the boundary of land once owned by the railway. You may well have walked over this one; there are others about to the sharp eyed.

Hippodrome

Mr. P. Ghillyer remembers the late Len Jeffrey who was the Chief Operator at the Hippodrome which was originally built as a Variety Theatre in 1902. It later changed to being a cinema. G. Prance was the well known manager of this building, well beloved by the people of Devonport.

Jimmy Hearn, well known to the people at Devonport Carnival, for the lovely miniature stage coach and two delightful Shetland ponies that gave children a ride around the oval for a penny (proceeds to charity) used to allow the coach and ponies to appear on the Hippodrome Variety Theatre during pantomimes.

Mr. P. Ghillyer remembers giving Sunday "Go as you please" concerts with Ted Tout, senior. These included anyone who wished to perform, civilian or anyone from the three services.

Argyle in 1930

Mrs. Kathleen Mills, neé Ketteridge of Devonport, was in the group that helped to celebrate promotion to the second division. The team started off the season in a canter with a wonderful run of success. Not until Christmas Day at Coventry did they meet their first reverse. Promotion was assured at Newport on Easter Monday with five games to spare. On 31st May, 1930, a triumphal tour of the city was made by the Argyle team when it seemed that the whole population turned out to express their jubilation.

1946 Football Team

The pitch was situated on the waste ground at the rear of the old N.F.S. (National Fire Service) building that once stood on the corner in Molesworth Road. A condition of joining the team was to attend the Belmont (Youth) Club and divine service once a week. One game played was against prisoners-of-war team in Central Park. Back: Roy Harris, Ken Williams, Ken Steer and Raymond Billings. Front: Raymond Haley, Ken Rowe, E. J. Lillicrap (on leave from the Army).

Johnstone Terrace in 1914

Mrs. Bright's family of 5 York Road is the longest living family on the Weston Mill estate, once known as Sir John Jackson's estate, which was built for the workers in the Dockyard. Her mother, Violet Irene Prowse, who at 16 years of age is in this photograph with Mary Jane Prowse, her grandmother. The tram to Keyham will bring back memories. She remembers her great grandfather, William Frost, who used to sing hymns all the way from Tamerton Foliot to the Dockyard

Coronation Celebrations 1953

The people of Devonport put on all kinds of local events for this Royal occasion, one being a fancy dress parade by the youngsters of Renown Street. The local bobby watches on while the contestants assemble for the photographer. Unfortunately no names have come forward for these but you may recognise some yourself.

Sheep are Safely Grazing

Not far from the spot where the sheep are grazing, two tigers escaped from a circus in a marquee in Devonport Brickfields about 1930. The whole of the city council had been invited as guests. The animals were loose in the Brickfields and one was reported to be roaming into Devonport Park.

Across the road a train would often pass along the open track along King's Road to the Southern Station (where the College of Further Education now stands), having travelled from Ocean Quay.

Busy Corner

Mrs. Bright remembers the Devonport Secondary (later High) School for Girls had their school on the ground level and first floor of the Technical School. The Foulston built Albermarle Villas nearby was for girl boarders and a part of the original school. She remembers seeing the men at work in the basement of the building. Devonport High School had their present premises in 1937. During the war, the French soldiers could be seen wearily marching past this spot having left the train in the Southern Station.

Family Group in 1948

Marjorie's (Britannia) father is on the left. Marjorie's little girl, Sylvia, is in front of him, and her mother is on Sylvia's left. Marjorie is standing behind her son, Arthur. Her husband is standing behind her Great Aunt who was the headmistress of York Street Infants.

Britannia Rules!

Mrs. Marjorie Laxton is Britannia. It was taken at York Street Infant's School, Devonport, 1910. The School's headmistress was her great aunt, Miss Minnie Holmes. Others in the photo are: John Evans, right of Britannia, and Hannah Mitchell, extreme right.

Generation Gap

Britannia's mother is in the 3rd row from the front and is wearing a lace collar. If Britannia is now in her 70s any guesses as to when this photograph of York Street Infants was taken? Britannia's Great Aunt, who later became headmistress of York Street Infants, is standing on the left of the photo.

Concert Party

The lawn, at the Vicarage of St. James the Great Church, which was situated on the opposite side of the road from the Dockyard wall and halfway between Albert and St. Levan Gates, was the venue in the photograph for a Morice Town School Concert Party. Boys and girls, too, from Saint James the Great Junior School sang songs such as "Old Father Thames," on the lawn.

Ford Infant's School, 1920

Mr. Gordon Scantlebury, of Waverley Road, St. Budeaux, is the second from the left in the top row. The boy holding the number in the front is believed to be Fred Wetherdon. On his right is Gordon Lusmore and on the extreme left is Rosie Dyer. Edna Campbell is 5th from the left in the 3rd row from the front (now Mrs. Williams).

Ford School, 1950

One of the many classes of local children are shown here whose education came under the headship of Mr. Johnson. Although the children have not been named, many people will almost certainly identify faces and recall pleasant memories of three decades ago.

Morice Town School Swimmers, 1936

When teachers were not on hand to pay the entrance fee into the new baths, boys such as Arthur Barker, standing extreme left, would swim from the free "Old Baths" for men and boys and mingle with those who had paid to enjoy the amenities such as a diving board in the new swimming baths.

King Street and Military School, about 1929

This school for boys and girls was renamed in 1930 to King Street Council School. Here are P. Glanville, F. Jones, R. Lock, C. Evans, J. White, A. Hines, F. Burlace, J. Burt, J. Warren, F. Rice, F. Ball, G. Stidwell, P. Webb, J. Lewis, Miss Barker, T. Holland, J. Buck, R. Sleep, R. Hardie, T. Hingston, J. Clough, G. Lucas, G. Arscott, T. Cann, J. Leach, P. Davy, F. Williams, Miss Chandler, headmistress, J. Watters, A. Allen, W. Watters, G. Minze, R. Watkins and A. Gould with others.

Devonport Central Hall Boating Club, 1932

A very active programme of rowing took members of the club all around the Plymouth area. Tidal movements usually determined the course either up the Tamar one week then one to Rame head and the Breakwater the next. This group was taken at Sellars Beach, on the River Yealm, comprising of W. White, E. Kingdom, A. Anderson, A. Browning, A. Rogers, A. Kitts, E. Sutton, R. Watkins, L. Bennett, Chiswell, C. Chiswell, N. Murray, R. Couzins, R. Westlake, A. Thompson and B. Sutton.

Morice Square Children About 1920

This large group of children form part of the Sunday School scholars of that area posed close to the corporation buildings. William Wotters and Frank Burlace have been identified but I have not met with success with the others. Can you help?

George Street

The *Half-moon*, on the left, and *King's Arms*, on the right, form a "gateway" to one of the finest sights in the world. A few yards further and one is able to stand by the Captain Scott memorial and look out to sea. Mrs. Laxton remembers living at 40 George Street next to the ballroom of Hamoaze House and as a girl being fascinated by the carriages and horses bringing some very regal-like persons to the social occasions.

William Street

Morice Town's principal thoroughfare looking towards Martin Terrace at the beginning of the century. On the right above the awning are the three brass balls denoting one of the numerous pawnbroker shops. Here at a later date was built the "Morice Town Picture House" about 1903. One set of tram lines ran up to the Royal Fleet Club. Double lines were laid in 1910. Twelve pubs, four eating houses and three workmen's dining rooms produced an unforgettable atmosphere.

Demolition of St. Mary's Church, 1959

St. Mary the Virgin, in James Street, was demolished in February, 1959. This beautiful building was well loved by the people in the vicinity and what the blitz failed to do was accomplished by a re-organisation plan to amalgamate certain churches. Others that met a similar end under merger plans were St. John the Baptist, in John Street, St. Stephen, George Street and St. James the Great in Keyham Road.

A DEVONPORT street is to commemorate a man who was known as "the saint of Devonport." He was the Rev. George Anselm Bennett, who for 31 years was the incumbent of St. Mary's Parish, Devonport.

Mr. Bennett is dead, and his church has been demolished, but one of the new streets to be built in the Ker-street redevelopment area is to be named Bennett-street.

It will run northwards from Mount-street to the new line of James-street west of the Guildhall.

This memorial to which the City Council has consented is in response to a petition organised by Mrs. L. M. Hooper, of 33, Ker-street, and signed by about 400 residents in the parish.

In wheel chair

For five years before the destruction of St. Mary's Church, Mr. Bennett was a victim of poliomyelitis, but in his wheel chair he was always present at evensong.

A bachelor, Mr. Bennett was not only outstanding as a scholar, but was indefatigable in parish work and many fine men acknowledge his work among them when they were boys.

The late Rev. George Bennett.

He was known by practically everyone in the parish and fought hard to save the church which had to go when the parish was incorporated in that of St. Aubyn.

A Faithful Servant

Many people remember with affection the life long devotion of the Rev. George Bennett to Devonport. This extract from the newspaper tells part of his long story and the tribute made to his memory in naming a local street after him.

Farewell to St. Mary's Church

This group photograph records the last occasion of the various officers of the church just before its closure and subsequent demolition. Mrs. L. Hooper, of George Street, is at the back; she was one of those who worked hard to prevent its closure but without success. Others here are Bob Austin, Arthur McLean, Mr. May, Frank Lang, Mr. Leonard Short, church reader, Michael McLean, Harry Dendle and Norah Eals.

Death Throes of St. Mary's

This photograph was taken on the 18th April, 1959, by Mrs. L. Hooper. The Rev. J. H. Jones was inducted at St. Aubyn Church to become Vicar of what was once five parishes, including St. Mary's. Objections to the demolition was put by Mr. Henry C. Gendle, the church council secretary, argued that it should be preserved because of its history, structure and ecclesiastical beauty.

St. John the Baptist

St. John's was damaged by enemy action. It was converted for use as a community centre by the Dockland Settlement. It was possible in the dark days of the "blackout" to enjoy oneself by learning ballroom dancing in its large hall. Devonport library is on the extreme right. The cobbled stones of Ker Street are in the foreground.

Old Presbyterian Church

This was one of Devonport's many fine churches which survived the blitz but fell to the developments of later years. It was demolished in 1972 having served the community. It stood in Duke St. Ope on the opposite side of the road to the Devonport Library, of late years the Motor Taxation Office.

Opening of Devonport Park, 1895

Wall plaques and memorials can be a great source of local information. This tells us about some "firsts" for the park and the tablet is still in position on the walls of the ornamented house there.

The Crucifix will be Removed

Because of pressure from a group, the crucifix was taken down from St. Stephens Church (the poorest parish in Devonport) and later found on Chelston Meadow tip. Situated in George Street, its side in Clowance Street, a part of Fort Street can be seen on the right of picture. The Church was badly damaged by enemy action and was demolished in 1959. The parishioners merged with St. Aubyn's parish.

North Corner About 1910

Some of Devonport's first houses were built here of wood construction. Robert Hay, a Royal Navy deserter, went into hiding here from the dreaded press gangs. He described what he saw from his window: "Waterman's skiffs, merchantmen's yawls, pinnances, cutters, warships, launches, gigs, landing all the time". In happier moments many Devonport families have embarked on pleasure trips from the pontoon bridge. This open view of the vicinity shows what a thriving spot it was with the various boats and men ready for work.

Arthur L. Clamp – the man behind the books

Arthur Leslie Clamp was a man of boundless energy with a passion for helping others, particularly through his love of history. A printer by trade, he started his career in a printing company before moving his family from Exeter to Plymouth to teach at the Plymouth College of Art and Design, where he eventually became the Head of the Printing Department.

A Devoted Family Man

Arthur with his five children.

Despite his love of teaching, Arthur prioritised his family, always making it home by 5:30pm for tea. He and his wife, Rosemary, raised five children: Susan, Angela, Elizabeth, David, and Steven. Arthur would often combine his love of family and history by taking his children on Sunday walks, encouraging them to appreciate historical monuments by taking photos or making crayon rubbings of gravestones for his books. The family home at 203 Elburton Road was a hub of activity, with a large garden, featuring a two-storey fort and a makeshift swimming pool.

A Lifelong Learner and Adventurer

Arthur's thirst for knowledge extended beyond history to a deep curiosity about the world. He was passionate about exploring different cultures, traditions, and cuisines, often taking advantage of his long summer holidays as a teacher to travel to places like India, Russia, South America, the middle east and the USA, sometimes bringing one of his children along. This adventurous spirit even influenced his home life, as seen by the short-lived family tradition of steam-cooking vegetables after a trip to Iceland.

History is a prominent feature of family days out

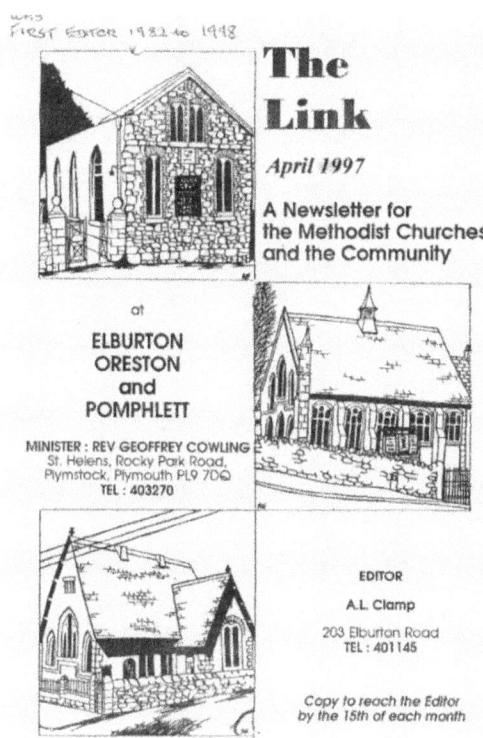

Community and Philanthropic Spirit

His commitment to serving others was evident in his long-standing involvement with the Elburton Methodist Church. He was the Sunday School Superintendent for over 15 years and served as the editor of the wider church's monthly newsletter, "The Link," for a similar duration. After Rosemary's very sad passing, Arthur later remarried and, following a chance encounter with a professor from India, established a connection with a missionary school in Chennai. Together with his new wife, Christine, he co-founded a "Sponsor a Child's Education" program that continues to this day.

Pictured left – The cover of 'The Link' complete with hand drawn sketches of each church by Angela
Below right – Arthur Clamp promoting his latest book
Below left – Arthur at home with his first wife, Rosemary
Below centre – Arthur on holiday with his second wife, Christine

A Legacy of Learning and Positivity

Arthur's greatest passion was history, which he brought to life through tireless research, documentation, and the many books he authored. He was driven by a need to "never be stuck in a rut," constantly seeking new experiences, meeting new people, and expanding his knowledge. With a positive attitude and a great sense of humour, he was always ready to help others, leaving a lasting impact on his family and community. His children, Susan, Angela, Elizabeth, David, and Steven, remember him with love and gratitude.

David Clamp, 2025

A Legacy of Local History

Below is the story of how Arthur L Clamp began writing books, in his own words, drafted shortly before he passed away in 2001. I have only made minor alterations to this text, correcting grammatical errors that he did not survive to correct himself. When I first discovered this text, I was shocked to see my name mentioned. It seems that, unbeknownst to me, I shared my first PC with him. I suspect he used it during the day when I was at school, although I do have one memory of sitting with him and showing him how it worked. It has been a pleasure to pick up where he left off and see his books republished and redistributed, and to know that I was part of the story, even back then. It was also fascinating to discover that his pricing structure matches the way I have tried to price the books, with a third going to local sellers and the rest covering printing costs with a little left over for my expenses.

I am his eldest grandson, and it is a privilege to curate his legacy, which we are calling 'The Clamp Collection'. The very last line of the text originally reads "The following pages list all the titles." Sadly, that page is missing and we have no record of all the books he published and knowing that some of those were researched by other authors makes the process of finding them even harder. I look forward to one day completing the collection and seeing them all available again. And maybe, one day, I'll even start writing my own to add to the series. For now, here is his story in his own words.

Steven Gibson, 2025

Writing and Publishing Booklets on Local Topics and Areas

I started this interest in either 1968 or 1969 when living in Woodford. I had by these dates established the Department of Printing and I think I must have been looking for something different to do. The first titles were of A5 size proofed from type set at Clarke, Doble and Brendon, Ltd., Plymouth printers, and then made up into pages and printed at Sawtell and Neilson, Ltd., Totnes.

Then began a slow process of getting them out to shops, etc. which proved to be more time consuming and difficult than actually researching, writing and getting the books into print. However, I persisted and opened a business account with Barclays Bank on the Broadway. I was advised to give it a title so I called it "Westway Publications". There came along another problem, one of storage of paper and finished books which was solved when the family moved to Elburton in 1970.

I changed the printer to Penwell, Ltd., Callington, Cornwall, as he was then just setting up himself and his prices seemed very reasonable. I did not get any of the printers to make up the complete books. I hand folded the flat printed sheets, stitched the books on a small manual table stitcher and trimmed them in a small hand turned guillotine which I bought from someone in Penzance for £40. It was brought up in a van.

The trouble and time going to and fro to Callington was too much so I transferred the printing to PDS Printers, Prince Rock, Plymouth, and I have been with them ever since. Now they are at Plympton which is easy to reach and they fold the flat sheets which was turning out to be a long chore which only saved a small part of the printing costs.

All my first titles were written by myself. I took the photographs and developed them in the loft of the house, the type was set by now on a computer situated in the house at Elburton from which I had collected photographic lengths of text to cut up and law down as pages.

At some point I decided that I would do my own film processing of lith film so I bought a large second hand process camera from Kingsbridge and learnt through trial and error to make line negatives of the text and halftone negatives of the illustrations which proved more difficult than I anticipated. The main problem was trying to keep the developer in the large dish at the correct temperature as any change would affect the developing time. I replaced this old camera with a brand new one bought from Croydon, Surrey, costing £900. This has turned out to be a great asset cutting out an expensive part of the printer's costs and one crucial aspect of the work which I could control.

By the middle 1970s there were many outlets I had contacted in Plymouth, up to Dartmoor, Exeter, around to Torbay, Totnes, Dartmouth and the South Hams. The market for local books was much greater than I had first thought and through getting to know many local people undertaking research themselves had the chance to help and make up books for other people who had in most instances, got together a collection of photographs with some text in a rather muddled way. Through my experience in print I was able to shape up their work and get it into print and in every case I had to pay the printer and let the person have the royalties. In the majority of titles produced in this manner this was another way of producing titles and it did give some profit to my work. However, I must say that in a few cases I lost out by either the other person getting the numbers wrong, not returning any monies from stock I delivered or they thought that more of their books should have been sold.

The print run was usually 1,000 copies and from time to time I have had reprints of 250 copies. It took about ten years to clear the first print run so I always had large stocks in the garage, workshop, etc. The numbers sold during the early years was about 7,000 copies a year increasing to around 9,000 copies and for the whole of the enterprise about 500,000 have been sold. The booklets have become part of the local scene and many people collect them, shops regularly order copies and I go around certain areas month by month restocking or replacing titles as necessary.

During the past year or so I have started setting the text on a Packard Bell PC, something which I should have done some years back. I share it with Steven Gibson, my grandson. There appears to be no end to the market for local books, but I could not earn a regular income because of the long time it takes to sell stock.

However, now exceeding 100 titles made up mainly of A4 twenty-four page booklets, some folded guides, with selling prices set with a third going to the shop which is the trade custom, the original idea has been quite successful and could go on for ever.

Apart from monetary benefits, however spasmodically these might be, I have learnt a lot myself, met many interesting people and have become part of the local scene with requests to give talks and to advise people about getting into print.

Arthur L Clamp, 2001

Death of local historical author

'He was an incredible character who was just loved by everybody who knew him'

This newspaper article, published by the Evening Herald on 17th August 2001, forms a good record of his life. Just as he encourages us to learn more about local history, we encourage you to learn a little about him. For that reason, we have included these pages at the back of all the most recently republished books, in honour of his memory and recognition of his contribution to the community.

www.ingramcontent.com/pod-product-compliance
Lightning Source LLC
Chambersburg PA
CBHW061406070526
44584CB00031B/4177